Andrew Jackson: Our Seventh
President
Ann Graham Gaines
AR B.L.: 5.5
Points: 1.0

ANDREW *Jackson*

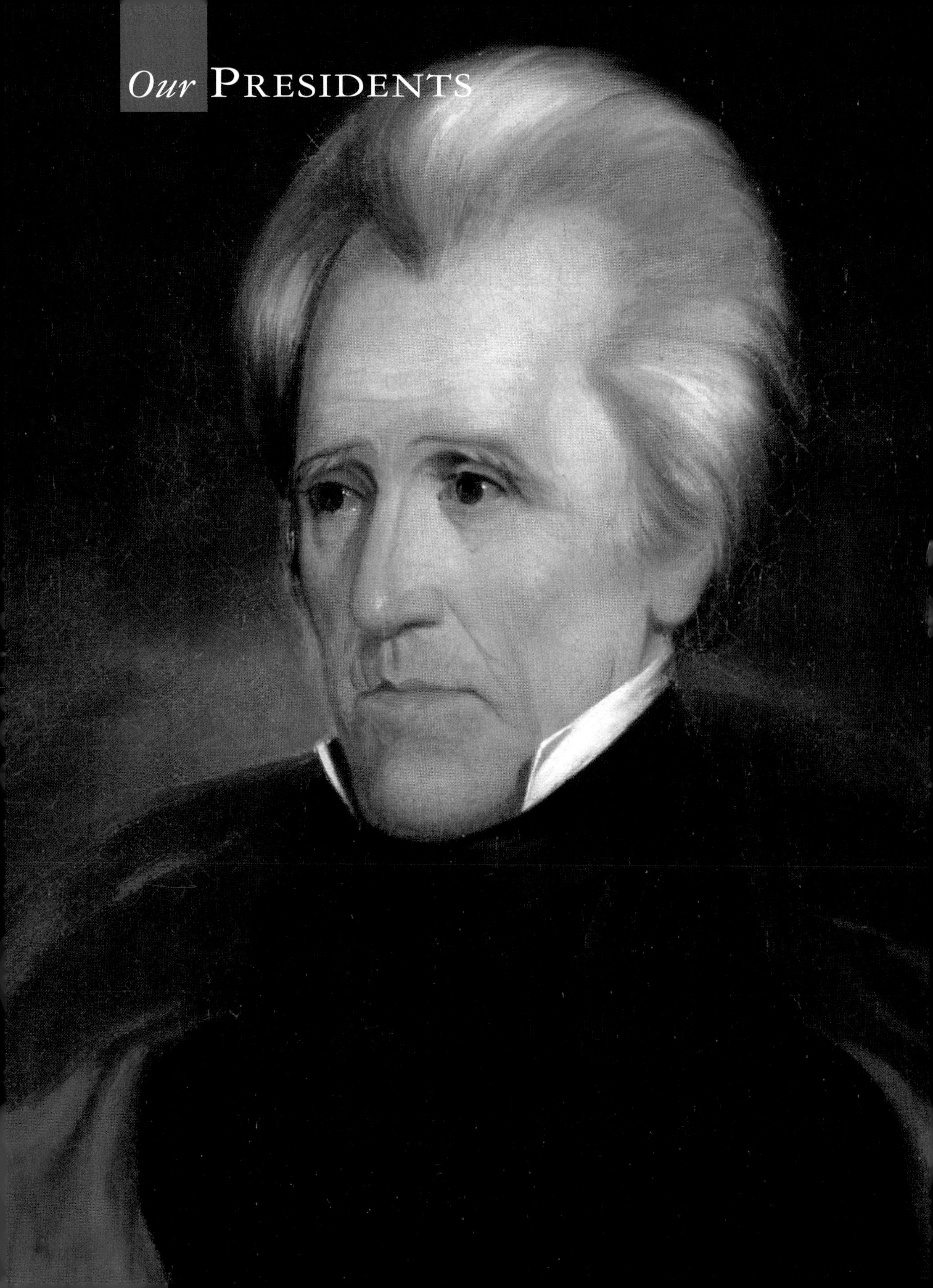

ANDREW *Jackson*

OUR SEVENTH PRESIDENT

By Ann Graham Gaines

SPIRIT
of America®

The Child's World®
Chanhassen, Minnesota

8

ANDREW *Jackson*

Published in the United States of America by The Child's World®
PO Box 326 • Chanhassen, MN 55317-0326 • 800-599-READ • www.childsworld.com

Acknowledgments

The Creative Spark: Mary Francis-DeMarois, Project Director; Elizabeth Sirimarco Budd, Series Editor;
Robert Court, Design and Art Direction; Janine Graham, Page Layout; Jennifer Moyers, Production

The Child's World®: Mary Berendes, Publishing Director; Red Line Editorial, Fact Research;
Cindy Klingel, Curriculum Advisor; Robert Noyed, Historical Advisor

Photos

Cover: White House Collection, courtesy White House Historical Association Bettmann/Corbis: 25, 34;
©Peter Harholdt/CORBIS: 13; Courtesy of The Hermitage: 6, 9, 14, 15, 21, 23, 30, 36, 37; Historic
Hudson Valley, Tarrytown, New York: 12; The Huntington Library, San Marino, California: 29; Library
of Congress Collections: 7, 10, 11, 17, 18, 20, 22, 26, 28, 33, 35; ©Sam Holland, Courtesy of the South
Carolina State House: 8; Woolaroc Museum, Bartlesville, Oklahoma: 27

Registration

The Child's World®, Spirit of America®, and their associated logos are the sole property and
registered trademarks of The Child's World®.

Library of Congress Cataloging-in-Publication Data

Gaines, Ann.
    Andrew Jackson : our seventh president / Ann Graham Gaines.
        p. cm.
    Includes bibliographical references and index.
    ISBN 1-56766-847-X (lib. bdg. : alk. paper)
    1. Jackson, Andrew, 1767–1845—Juvenile literature. 2. Presidents—United States—Biography—
Juvenile literature. [1. Jackson, Andrew, 1767–1845. 2. Presidents.] I. Title.
    E382 .G24 2001
    973.5'6'092—dc21

                                                        00-011494

Contents

Chapter ONE

Southern Childhood

Andrew Jackson had a difficult childhood. Unlike the six presidents who served before him, he was born poor. By age 14, he had lost his entire family to war and illness.

ANDREW JACKSON'S FAMILY WAS DIFFERENT from those of other early presidents. They were poor people who came from Ireland to start a new life in America. His father was a farmer, also named Andrew Jackson. His mother's name was Elizabeth, but people called her Betty.

The Jacksons settled in a tiny town called Waxhaw in South Carolina. There they bought 200 acres of land. Before Andrew Jackson's father could plant crops, there was much work to be done. He had to chop down many trees to make way for planting. One day early in the spring of 1767, he tried to move a heavy log out of a field. It was too big for him to move alone. He strained his heart and collapsed. By nighttime, he was dead.

Jackson was the first president to be born in a log cabin. From his difficult childhood in South Carolina, he grew up to become a tough, courageous man known for his bad temper.

The Jacksons already had two little boys, Hugh and Robert. Just a few days after her husband died, Betty Jackson gave birth to Andrew, the future president. He was born on March 15, 1767. As a child, Andrew was a tall, thin redhead who liked to run and jump. He loved to ride horses, too.

By the time he was five years old, Andrew knew how to read. He went to a school for little children in Waxhaw. He would always be very smart. But even though he was good at math and reading, grammar and spelling were difficult for him.

The American **Revolution** began in 1775 in the northern **colonies** of New England.

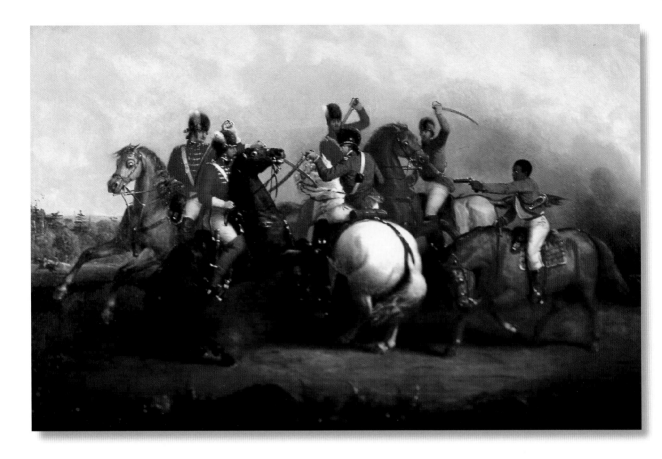

Although the American Revolution began in New England, battles were fought in the South as well. The Battle of Cowpens, shown here, took place in South Carolina. A force of 1,000 Americans won a huge victory against the British, eventually forcing them to withdraw from the area.

The people who lived in South Carolina knew all about the war. But for a long time, the fighting took place far away from them. Andrew's older brother, Hugh, joined the American army. He died in battle in 1779.

In 1780, a British general named Charles Cornwallis sent soldiers into South Carolina. His army needed supplies. He had ordered his men to take items such as food and hay. Members of local **militias** gathered near Waxhaw. They were preparing to fight the invaders. Suddenly, a huge force of British soldiers surprised them. About 100 of the **patriots,** including many of the Jacksons' friends and neighbors, died in the fighting that followed. Some patriots were shot in battle, but others gave up. They thought the British soldiers would make them prisoners of war. Instead, the patriots were killed.

When news of the battle reached the Jacksons, Betty took Robert and Andrew to the town's church. There they helped care for Americans who were wounded in the battle.

This frightening event became known as the Waxhaw Massacre. After it was over, the Jacksons and other residents of the area fled to North Carolina. A few weeks later, they were able to return home. Both Robert and Andrew were furious at the British soldiers' treatment of their friends and neighbors during the Waxhaw Massacre. The brothers joined the American army. They were assigned to the cavalry, the part of the army that fought on horseback. Robert was 16 years old. Many boys his age fought in the American Revolution. He was trained and went into battle. Andrew was just 13 years old and still too young to fight, so he worked as a messenger.

As a boy, Andrew Jackson was a wild redhead with lots of energy. He loved to ride horses and roughhouse. His family worried that he might hurt himself one day because he was so reckless.

Interesting Facts

▶ When Jackson was a boy, many adults in his hometown could not read. People who could read recited newspaper articles, important documents, and short stories to crowds. Jackson became a reader when he was just nine years old. One thing he read to the people of his town was the Declaration of Independence.

In April of 1781, both Jackson boys went home to visit their mother in South Carolina. During their visit, British soldiers captured them. One soldier ordered the boys to clean his boots. When they refused, he slashed them with his sword. With terrible wounds, Andrew and Robert were sent to a prison in New Jersey. The conditions were terrible in the prison, and both boys became ill.

Betty Jackson traveled to New Jersey, hoping she could help her sons. She went to see the commander in charge of the prison. She begged for the release of her sons and

When Andrew Jackson was 14, he and his brother were taken prisoner by the British. When an officer ordered them to clean his boots, they bravely refused. As punishment, the British soldier cut the boys with his sword.

10

three other boys from Waxhaw. The commander agreed to let her take the boys home. Unfortunately, Robert was so ill that he died just two days after they reached home. Andrew was strong enough to recover from the disease.

Close to the end of the war, Betty Jackson went to Charleston, South Carolina, as a nurse. The British allowed her to board prison ships and care for injured and sick American soldiers. Unfortunately, Betty became sick while caring for the men, and she also died. Andrew Jackson, at age 14, had lost his family. He was all alone.

In December of 1784, at 17 years old, Andrew left Waxhaw. He was still tall and skinny, but he was also very strong. He was wild by nature, but he now dreamed of achieving something important with his life. In Salisbury, North Carolina, he began to study law. Within two years, Andrew Jackson was a lawyer.

During the American Revolution, the British army kept some of its American prisoners on ships like this one, called the Jersey. *It was difficult to escape from these ships, and the conditions were terrible. A thousand men and boys were crammed into a small space. There was very little food. Lice and rats pestered the prisoners and spread disease. About 11,000 Americans died of disease and starvation on the* Jersey *during the Revolution.*

Chapter TWO

A Nation's Hero

This portrait of Andrew Jackson was painted when he was about 40 years old. After working as a lawyer for many years, Jackson joined the army. He was such a good leader that he was made a general.

BY THE TIME ANDREW JACKSON WAS GROWN, many Americans were packing their belongings and heading west. When Europeans first came to North America, settlers had found the Appalachian Mountains difficult to cross. This rugged mountain range runs for hundreds of miles from New York south to Alabama and Georgia.

Later, hunters discovered the Cumberland Gap. The Gap is a low place where it is easy to travel across the mountains. Native Americans and animals had been using it for thousands of years. Soon Americans began to pack their belongings and head west to Kentucky and lands beyond. Between 1775 and 1810, more than 200,000 settlers headed through the Gap to what was then the far West of the

United States. Andrew Jackson, eager for adventure, was among these settlers.

Jackson had always wanted to see the West. He was pleased when the North Carolina **legislature** sent him to its western **frontier** to work as a lawyer. North Carolina was much bigger than it is today. It stretched all the way to the Mississippi River. But soon its western part would become a new state, called Tennessee.

In 1769, pioneer Daniel Boone cleared a road through the Cumberland Gap, opening the West to American settlers. Andrew Jackson was among the thousands who moved west to start a new life.

13

Jackson went from one frontier settlement to another, traveling on horseback to his destinations. In each new town, he argued a case in court. After a few years, he stopped traveling and settled in a small town called Nashville. Jackson opened his own law office there and began to earn money. His clients often paid him with land instead of cash. Jackson also bought land as he earned more money.

In 1791, Jackson married Rachel Robards. Years later, they turned a piece of their land into a plantation, a large farm where they grew crops such as cotton and corn. They called it "The Hermitage." At first the Jacksons lived in a log cabin. Later they hired workers to build a big, beautiful house. Jackson also had been buying slaves. He put them to work planting fields of cotton. Rachel and Andrew Jackson never had any children of their own, but in 1809, they adopted a little boy. They named him Andrew Jackson Jr.

As a lawyer, Jackson learned a lot about government and the law. As time went by, he decided he wanted to become a politician. Then he would be involved in creating new laws for the country. In 1796, Jackson became the first person from Tennessee elected to the House of Representatives. The next year, he was elected senator. But in 1798, he went back to Tennessee to become a judge. He also became an officer in the state militia. By 1802,

This log cabin is the first home that the Jacksons built on their plantation, which they called The Hermitage. Many years later, they built a beautiful mansion to replace the cabin.

15

Jackson had become a major general in the militia. He commanded many volunteer soldiers, training them to be prepared for Native American attacks. He soon became well known for his temper. When others made him angry, he would challenge them to duels, which are gunfights used to settle arguments.

In 1806, Jackson retired from his position as a judge. He wanted to devote his attention to his plantation. Soon, however, he would work for his country as a military leader.

For many years, British ships had been stopping American ships at sea to keep the United States from trading its goods with other nations. American leaders demanded that the British government stop interfering with American trade, but it refused. In 1812, the United States declared war on Great Britain. Jackson decided to leave his plantation and fight for his country. He became commander of the entire Tennessee militia. Jackson and his troops won many victories against the Native Americans, who were helping the British.

By April of 1814, the U.S. Army had made Jackson a general. A month later, he

The United States declared war on Great Britain in 1812. Andrew Jackson left his plantation to fight as a general in the U.S. Army. He understood that if Americans lost the war, it could threaten their independence. Great Britain might attempt to take over the country.

became commander of all American troops in Tennessee, Mississippi, and Louisiana. When British soldiers attacked Alabama, Jackson's men fought back and forced them to **retreat.** When the British fled to Florida, they were forced to retreat yet again.

In December of 1814, Jackson and his men went to New Orleans. Americans feared the British would soon attack that city. If they succeeded, they could block trade on the Mississippi River, leaving Americans short of supplies. The American soldiers went to help protect the city.

Soon after Jackson arrived, the British began to attack towns in southern Louisiana.

Jackson's victory at the Battle of New Orleans made him a national hero. It also meant that a foreign power would never again control the Mississippi River Valley. People were so proud of Jackson's victory that they hoped he would run for president one day.

On January 8, 1815, they attacked Jackson and his men. He beat them easily in the Battle of New Orleans. Americans rejoiced when they got the news of his victory. By this time, they also found out the war had ended. In Europe, representatives of the United States and Great Britain had agreed to peace on December 24, 1814, but word had been slow to travel across the Atlantic Ocean.

Jackson was a national hero. He was known as a smart, courageous man and a great general, one who also had a bad temper at times. Few people knew that he was also devoted to his family and kind to his friends.

For a time, Jackson went home to his wife and son at The Hermitage. But new problems were brewing between U.S. citizens and the Native Americans of the South. At the time, Spain still controlled Florida. The Seminoles were a Native American tribe that moved back and forth between Spanish Florida and American Georgia. They were angry because Americans were settling on their land. To scare them away, the Seminoles raided American settlements. From camps in Florida, they rode across the border into Georgia. The tribe killed a few Americans and burned their property.

The American army announced it was going to stop the Native American raids. In 1818, Jackson rejoined the army and took charge of the American soldiers in Georgia. After Native Americans killed some of his troops, Jackson was angry. He did not wait for government orders to tell him what to do. Instead, he and his men marched into Florida. They battled and beat the Seminoles and captured Spanish forts.

Interesting Facts

▸ Once in a duel, Jackson's opponent fired first, hitting him in the chest. With blood filling his shoes, Jackson calmly took aim and shot the man dead.

▸ During the War of 1812, soldiers nicknamed Jackson "Old Hickory." They named him after this hard, rugged wood because he was so strong and tough.

▸ The Seminoles still live in Florida, even though the U.S. government tried to drive them out.

Jackson was sent to Georgia because the Seminoles had been attacking U.S. settlements and forts. But he did much more than stop the Indian raids. He marched his men into Spanish Florida, took it over, and then claimed it for the United States.

Although some Americans thought Jackson should be punished for acting without orders, President James Monroe did not have him arrested. Jackson's actions later helped the United States. Spain's leaders wanted to avoid more trouble, so they agreed to give all of Florida to the United States. Not all American leaders were happy with Jackson, however. Some did not like the fact that he had taken such an enormous amount of power into his own hands.

ANDREW JACKSON'S WIFE WAS NAMED Rachel. She was born in 1767 in Virginia. When she was 17, Rachel married her first husband, Lewis Robards. He had a mean temper and treated her badly. Rachel tried hard to be a good wife, but he was always jealous. He did not want her to speak to other men. If she did, he accused her of being unfaithful. When Rachel and Andrew Jackson became friends, Robards said terrible things about her. Jackson wanted to protect Rachel. In 1790, Rachel decided to leave Robards. She moved out of their house and back to her father's home. Friends told her that Robards had divorced her. When Andrew Jackson asked her to marry him, she happily said yes. Jackson was also a man well known for his temper, but Rachel was the love of his life. He treated her with great affection. Rachel was gentle and kind, and their marriage calmed Jackson's wild ways.

In 1793, Andrew and Rachel Jackson received bad news. They learned that Lewis Robards had never truly divorced her. A judge finally granted the divorce, so Rachel and Andrew had to marry a second time. When Andrew Jackson ran for president, his political enemies wanted to make him look as bad as they could. They spread a rumor that Rachel had been married to two men at one time. Rachel had never truly wanted Jackson to become the president, and the **campaign** was very difficult for her. The rumor upset and embarrassed her so much that she became ill. Soon after Jackson won the election, Rachel had a heart attack and died. Until the end of his life, Jackson talked about how much he missed his beloved wife.

21

Chapter THREE

Headed for the White House

Although many politicians were angered by Jackson's actions in Florida, President Monroe (above) named him governor of the new territory. Jackson did not stay there long, however. Soon he was angry that Monroe would not give him more power.

IN 1821, PRESIDENT MONROE ASKED ANDREW Jackson to become the governor of Florida. The Jacksons moved to Pensacola, the capital at that time. Jackson worked to build a new government. He divided the territory into counties and created a court system. But he became angry when Monroe ignored some of his recommendations. In fact, Jackson was so angry that he quit. He and Rachel went home to Tennessee.

Early in 1822, Americans started to talk about who would run for president in 1824. Many people wanted Jackson to become a **candidate.** But first, he was reelected to the Senate. He returned to Washington, D.C. in 1823. When he was not working in the Senate, he was campaigning for the presidency.

After leaving Florida in 1821, Jackson spent a short time at The Hermitage. In 1823, he returned to Washington, D.C., after he was once again elected a U.S. senator.

Four men ran for president in 1824—John Quincy Adams, Henry Clay, William Crawford, and Andrew Jackson. Although most Americans wanted Jackson to be their new president, the **electoral college** had to cast their votes. Jackson received the most

▶ Many Americans were angry when John Quincy Adams became the president. The overwhelming majority of citizens wanted Jackson to lead the nation.

▶ Andrew Jackson read 20 newspapers a day to keep up on political news.

votes, but this did not make him the president. To win, he had to receive more than half the votes, and he did not.

According to the U.S. **Constitution,** the House of Representatives decides who will be president if a candidate does not receive a majority of the votes. Henry Clay was Speaker of the House, the leader of the House of Representatives. He was very powerful, and he was able to convince other representatives how to vote. In public, Clay did not say whom he wanted to be president. But behind closed doors, he told other politicians that he thought Jackson would make a poor leader. Clay believed Jackson would not cooperate with Congress. He thought Jackson would fight to achieve his own goals instead. Clay and John Quincy Adams met in secret. Clay agreed to help Adams win the House vote.

Thanks to Clay, John Quincy Adams won the election. Jackson and his supporters were outraged when Adams named Clay the secretary of state, one of the most important jobs in the president's **cabinet.** Jackson's supporters said that Adams and his friends did not follow the wishes of the American people but did as they pleased.

Jackson returned to Tennessee after Adams's **inauguration.** He was already thinking about the next election. He promised himself that next time, he would win no matter what. Many Americans still supported Jackson. Throughout the next four years, they criticized President Adams for the way Jackson had been treated.

Jackson attended a reception at the White House while Adams was president. At the time, Jackson had already begun campaigning to win the next election.

During Adams's term, Jackson and his supporters created a new **political party,** called the **Democrats.** Jackson's supporters wrote newspaper articles, explaining why people should vote for Democrats. They gave speeches to Americans, promising to help those who had less money. In the past, American politicians often listened only to what wealthy Americans wanted from the government. Americans with less money, such as shopkeepers and farmers, liked the Democratic Party. They believed the Democrats were interested in helping them instead of the rich.

Jackson began to campaign for the presidency three years before the election of 1828. John Quincy Adams was still the president, but many people began to support Jackson. His efforts paid off, and he won the election in a landslide—a huge number of votes! In 1829, Jackson was sworn in at what became known as "the people's inaugural." He promised to turn the government over to the common man. To prove it, he opened the White House to ordinary Americans for the first time. Thousands of people swarmed into the elegant mansion. It was a mess! Some people accidentally broke things, while others spit tobacco juice on the carpet. People even stood on the chairs and sofas to get a good look at the mansion. Jackson didn't mind. He knew the people were acting this way because they were happy he had been elected.

Although Jackson was pleased to be elected, it was a sad and difficult time for him. Just weeks after he won the election, his wife Rachel died. Jackson moved to Washington alone.

Jackson invited the American public to his inauguration. Thousands attended "the people's inauguration."

HISTORIANS OFTEN call Andrew Jackson "the people's president" because he was interested in the problems of ordinary Americans. He wanted people who were not wealthy to have a voice in American government. Andrew Jackson did not care about all Americans, however. He was a **racist** who believed that because of the color of their skin, white people were better than blacks and Native Americans. He did not think people of other races deserved equal rights.

In fact, Andrew Jackson believed that white Americans had the right to take away land where Native Americans had lived for hundreds of years. He talked Congress into passing a law that gave the president the right to use the army to "remove" Native Americans from lands that white settlers wanted. Soldiers forced Native Americans to travel west on what became known as the "Trail of Tears."

In 1836, the Creek tribe of Native Americans were attacked by militias in Georgia. The tribe's homes were destroyed, and people began to starve. A few went to white settlements to steal food for their families. This upset white people. They called for the army to take the Creeks away. Soldiers rounded them up and forced them to march west of the Mississippi.

The Cherokees chose to leave their homelands before soldiers made them go. Between 1835 and 1838, 16,000 Cherokees packed up everything they owned and left their homes. As many as 4,000 of them died on their trip west. Other tribes that were removed were the Chickasaws, the Choctaws, and the Seminoles.

Chapter FOUR

The President's Power

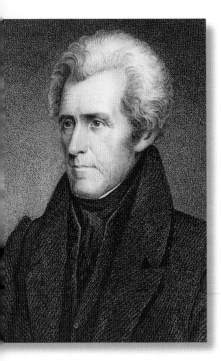

Although brokenhearted by the loss of his beloved wife, Jackson entered the presidency in 1829 determined to make big changes in the way the government worked.

ANDREW JACKSON SERVED TWO TERMS AS president. One of the first things he did was replace many government employees. He fired nearly 1,000 of the 10,000 people who then worked for the government. Some of those he fired had been accused of stealing money from the government. He also took positions away from people who had held their jobs for many years. He believed new employees would help make government offices run better. He said they would work harder and bring new ideas to their jobs. Jackson usually filled these positions with his own supporters, who would be sure to help him accomplish his goals.

Newspapers reported that there were now government jobs available. Many people wrote

or came to the White House, asking Jackson to hire them. Some of them were Democrats who had helped him get elected. Others were ordinary people looking for work as bookkeepers or secretaries. Jackson felt frustrated because he had to turn away many who wanted jobs. But this would be just one of the problems he would face during his presidency.

A serious issue had begun to divide the country, especially upsetting southerners.

When Jackson became president, the White House still sat in the middle of farmland. He had a stone wall and wooden fence built to surround the house and its grounds (shown above). To the far right is the Capitol building.

To Americans, President Jackson was still a great hero, and he was popular with the people. His strong will and determination to get his way often caused problems with other politicians, however.

The government gave large amounts of money to northern and western states to build roads and canals. The South did not need these things, so it received less government money. Southerners thought this was unfair. So did Jackson, who believed the **federal** government should only pay for projects that helped *all* Americans. Congress passed a **bill** that gave Kentucky money for a new road. Kentucky was considered a western state at the time. Southerners complained that others were still getting more than their fair share. Jackson refused to sign this bill, pleasing people in the South.

Southerners cheered Jackson yet again when he convinced Congress to pass the Indian Removal Act in 1830. This law said the president could order the army to move Native Americans off land that white Americans wanted.

30

White settlers in Georgia and Alabama wanted the Creek, Cherokee, and Choctaw tribes to leave their states, even though they had lived there for centuries. In 1832, the Supreme Court, the most powerful court in the country, said that Native Americans had a right to the land on which they lived. Jackson ignored the court. He continued to have Native Americans "removed."

Jackson also did something that made him *less* popular in the South. His vice president, John C. Calhoun, was from South Carolina. Calhoun did not like a **tariff** that Congress had created in 1828. It meant that Americans had to pay a special tax on many materials such as metals and fabrics, that were brought to the United States from other countries. The tariff made these items cost more, so that more people would buy American-made goods.

The southerners were against the tariff. They used more imported goods than other parts of the country, and they did not want to pay more for them. In addition, Great Britain bought cotton from the South to make into fabric and clothing. When Americans bought

31

less of these things from Great Britain, the British bought less cotton from the South.

Calhoun declared that his state would not pay the tariff. He believed that states had the right to nullify federal laws, which meant they could refuse to obey them. Jackson threatened to send troops to South Carolina to make its citizens obey the law. Calhoun finally backed down. Jackson then worked to lower the tariff. This matter left bad feelings between the North and South. Calhoun later stepped down as vice president and began to devote himself to helping the South.

In 1832, the next presidential election was held. Jackson ran for reelection, and Martin Van Buren ran as his vice president. Many Americans still believed the Democrats were interested in helping ordinary people, so Jackson and Van Buren won easily. Jackson had one major goal in his second term. He wanted to destroy the Second Bank of the United States, which was a private bank that held the government's money. He and his supporters thought the bank had grown too powerful. If it closed, smaller banks could be more successful.

Interesting Facts

▶ Andrew Jackson was the first president to ride a train while in office.

▶ In 1832, a doctor removed a bullet from Jackson's arm. It had been there for 20 years.

Jackson ordered that all the government's money be withdrawn from the Second Bank. The secretary of the **treasury** refused to obey his orders, so Jackson fired him. In September of 1833, the new secretary withdrew the money from the Second Bank.

The Senate was angry that Jackson had not asked them what to do. Its members decided Jackson had to be punished. They voted to censure him. When Congress censures the president, its members state formally that they believe he has done something wrong. Jackson replied by saying he did not have to do what

In 1816, the government gave the Second Bank of the United States the right to handle the country's money for the next 20 years. This meant the bank could print money whenever it wanted and make loans to whomever it wanted. It had great power over the country and its citizens. This cartoon shows President Jackson and Vice President Van Buren fighting a "many-headed monster" that symbolizes the bank.

Jackson and his vice president, Martin Van Buren (above), were close friends. They had founded the Democratic Party together and usually agreed on important issues. Jackson helped Van Buren win the election of 1836.

the Senate wanted. He believed his responsibility was to the American people, not to other politicians. The Second Bank finally closed its doors, as Jackson had wanted.

In 1836, the next presidential election was held. At the time, there was no law that said a president could serve only two terms. Andrew Jackson could have run a third time, but he was ill and decided against it. He was pleased when his vice president, Martin Van Buren, won the election. Jackson thought Van Buren would do a good job and continue the projects he had started. On March 4, 1837, Martin Van Buren was inaugurated as the eighth president of the United States.

Jackson went home to his beloved plantation in Tennessee. He had been away for a very long time, and his farm needed a lot of work. He bought new farm equipment and made repairs to his house. He ordered his slaves to plant new crops. For a time, Jackson remained interested in politics. Politicians wrote to him, and he offered them advice.

But he was growing weaker. By 1845, he was very sick. He had to spend most of his time in bed. Jackson realized that he would soon die.

On June 8, 1845, Andrew Jackson died at The Hermitage. He was 78 years old. Throughout his life, he fought hard to accomplish his goals. This fierce, stubborn man never let anyone stand in his way. As a general, he fought with all his might to protect the nation. As president, he wanted most of all to help ordinary Americans. In turn, the nation's people admired him. In the end, what mattered most to Jackson was his country. "I thank God that my life has been spent in a land of liberty," Jackson once said, "and that He has given me a heart to love my country with the affection of a son."

Shortly before he died, Jackson traveled to Nashville to pose for this photograph. Photography had just been introduced to the United States. Jackson posed in part because he was fascinated by the camera, which was a new invention. But he also had his picture taken out of pride. He wanted to leave Americans a final picture of himself.

WHEN HE WAS A YOUNG MAN, ANDREW JACKSON BOUGHT AND SOLD MANY pieces of land in the area around Nashville. In 1804, he found a place so beautiful, he wanted to live there forever. He turned the land into a plantation and called it The Hermitage. Jackson chose this name because a hermit is someone who goes off into the wilderness to live alone. He wanted The Hermitage to be a place where he and his wife Rachel could escape the cares of the world and enjoy peace and quiet. They lived in a small log cabin at The Hermitage for the first 17 years. Then they began building a brick house, where they moved in 1821. In 1834, a few years after Rachel died, the brick house burned down. Jackson built a beautiful new mansion, which still stands today.

Over the years, Andrew Jackson bought and sold many slaves. They lived on The Hermitage plantation in small log cabins. A few worked in Jackson's house, but most worked in his fields. They planted and tended huge fields of cotton and corn. They ran his cotton gin. They also took care of the plantation's livestock, especially the racehorses Jackson loved.

Andrew Jackson retired to The Hermitage when he left the presidency. He died there in 1845, and his son sold the plantation about 10 years later. Today it is open for visitors to tour and learn more about the nation's seventh president.

1765 Andrew Jackson's parents come to America from Ireland.

1767 Andrew Jackson's father dies in March. Andrew is born just a few days later on March 15.

1772 At age 5, Andrew Jackson has already learned to read. He starts to go to school.

1776 Andrew Jackson reads the Declaration of Independence to the people of his town.

1779 Hugh Jackson, the oldest of the Jackson boys, dies in battle.

1780 Local militia soldiers fight the British near the Jackson's home in what will become known as the Waxhaw Massacre. The Jackson family helps tend the wounded. After the battle, Andrew and his brother, Robert, join the American army.

1781 In April, the Jackson boys are captured by British soldiers and taken to prison. Their mother finally arranges for their release. Both boys are ill, and Robert dies as soon as they arrive home. Betty Jackson becomes ill and dies while nursing sick American prisoners of war. Andrew Jackson is the only surviving member of his family. He lives with relatives for the next three years.

1784 Jackson decides to study law.

1787 Jackson goes to western North Carolina to work as a lawyer. Eventually, he settles in Nashville, located in what will soon become the state of Tennessee. He opens his own law office.

1791 Jackson marries Rachel Robards.

1796 Jackson is elected to the U.S. House of Representatives.

1797 Jackson is elected to the U.S. Senate.

1798 Jackson becomes a judge in the state of Tennessee. He also becomes an officer in the Tennessee state militia.

1806 Jackson retires from his position as a judge and devotes his attention to The Hermitage, the plantation he and Rachel have built.

1809 Rachel and Andrew Jackson adopt a boy. They name him Andrew Jackson Jr.

1812 The United States declares war on Great Britain. The War of 1812 begins. Jackson joins the U.S. Army.

1814 The War of 1812 ends in December.

1815 Jackson becomes a national hero after he and his men beat the British in the Battle of New Orleans on January 8.

1818 Andrew Jackson leads American soldiers into Spanish Florida to fight the

Seminole War. Jackson is made a general and then commander of all American troops in Tennessee, Mississippi, and Louisiana.

1821 President James Monroe appoints Jackson governor of the new territory of Florida. Jackson quits before the year is over.

1822 Some Americans begin to encourage Jackson to run for president in the next election, which will be held in 1824.

1823 Jackson is once again elected to the Senate.

1824 Jackson receives the most popular votes in the presidential election. He does not become president., however, because he has not won a majority of votes in the electoral college. The House of Representatives votes for John Quincy Adams as president.

1825 Many Americans complain when Adams is sworn in as president. Jackson begins to campaign for the next election.

1828 Congress places tariffs on imported raw materials, angering many southerners. Jackson is elected president of the United States. His wife dies just weeks after his election.

1829 Almost immediately after he takes office, Jackson fires nearly 1,000 government employees. He gives many of the jobs to his supporters. Vice President Calhoun declares that the states can nullify federal laws believed to be unconstitutional.

1830 Jackson convinces Congress to pass the Indian Removal Act.

1832 Jackson ignores a Supreme Court ruling stating that Native Americans have a right to keep their land. He continues his Indian removal policy. Jackson is elected to a second term. His new vice president is Martin Van Buren. Jackson begins his fight to destroy the Second Bank of the United States, which he feels has become too powerful.

1833 All government money is withdrawn from the Second Bank. It is later forced to close.

1834 The Senate censures Jackson because it believes he had no right to remove money from the Second Bank without approval from Congress.

1836 Jackson refuses to run for president for a third term. His vice president, Martin Van Buren, is elected the eighth president of the United States.

1837 After Van Buren's inauguration, Jackson returns home to Tennessee.

1845 Andrew Jackson dies on June 8.

bill (BILL)
A bill is an idea for a new law that is presented to a group of lawmakers. When Congress passed a bill to pay for new roads in Kentucky, Jackson refused to sign it.

cabinet (KAB-ih-net)
A cabinet is the group of people who advise a president. The secretary of state is part of the president's cabinet.

campaign (kam-PAYN)
A campaign is the process of running for an election, including activities such as giving speeches or attending rallies. Jackson's first campaign was difficult for his wife.

candidate (KAN-dih-det)
A candidate is a person running in an election. Americans wanted Jackson to be a presidential candidate in the 1824 election.

colonies (KOL-uh-neez)
The Colonies were the American areas ruled by Great Britain before 1775. The colonies became the first 13 states of the United States.

constitution (kon-stih-TOO-shun)
A constitution is the set of basic principles that govern a state, country, or society. The U.S. Constitution says

the House of Representatives decides who will be president when no candidate wins a majority of votes.

Democrats (DEM-uh-kratz)
Democrats are members of the Democratic political party, one of the two major political parties in the United States. Jackson and his friends formed the Democratic Party.

electoral college (ee-LEKT-uh-rul KAWL-ij)
The electoral college is made up of representatives from each state who vote for candidates in presidential elections. Members of the electoral college cast their votes according to the candidate that most people in their state prefer.

federal (FED-er-ul)
Federal means having to do with the central government of the United States, rather than a state or city government. John Calhoun believed that states had the right to ignore federal laws.

frontier (frun-TEER)
A frontier is a region that is at the edge of or beyond settled land. As a young man, Jackson went to the western frontier to work as a lawyer.

Glossary TERMS

inauguration
(ih-nawg-yuh-RAY-shun)
An inauguration is the ceremony that takes place when a new presi-dent begins a term. Jackson's inauguration was known as "the people's inauguration."

legislature (LEJ-ih-slay-chur)
A legislature is the part of a government that makes laws. The North Carolina legislature sent Jackson to the West as a lawyer.

militias (muh-LISH-uhz)
Militias are volunteer armies, made up of citizens who have trained as soldiers. During the Revolution, militias were formed to fight the British.

patriots (PAY-tree-uts)
A patriot was any of the American colonists who wanted independence from Britain. As a young man, many of Jackson's friends and neighbors were patriots.

political party
(puh-LIT-ih-kul PAR-tee)
A political party is a group of people who share similar ideas about how to run a government. Jackson helped form the Democratic political party.

racist (RAY-sist)
A racist is a person who thinks his or her race is superior to others. Jackson was a racist because he believed white people were better than blacks and Native Americans.

retreat (ree-TREET)
If an army retreats, it moves back or withdraws to avoid danger or defeat. Jackson's men forced the British to retreat in several battles during the War of 1812.

revolution (rev-uh-LOO-shun)
A revolution is something that causes a complete change in government. The American Revolution was a war fought between the United States and Great Britain from 1775 to 1783.

tariff (TAR-iff)
A tariff is a tax on foreign goods. Southerners in the 1800s used many foreign goods, so they did not want tariffs on them.

treasury (TREZH-ur-ee)
A treasury manages a government's money, including its income and expenses. The secretary of the treasury is in charge of the government's money.

Our PRESIDENTS

President	Birthplace	Life Dates	Term	Political Party	First Lady
George Washington	Virginia	1732–1799	1789–1797	None	Martha Dandridge Custis Washington
John Adams	Massachusetts	1735–1826	1797–1801	Federalist	Abigail Smith Adams
Thomas Jefferson	Virginia	1743–1826	1801–1809	Democratic-Republican	widower
James Madison	Virginia	1751–1836	1809–1817	Democratic-Republican	Dolley Payne Todd Madison
James Monroe	Virginia	1758–1831	1817–1825	Democratic-Republican	Elizabeth "Eliza" Kortright Monroe
John Quincy Adams	Massachusetts	1767–1848	1825–1829	Democratic-Republican	Louisa Catherine Johnson Adams
Andrew Jackson	South Carolina	1767–1845	1829–1837	Democrat	widower
Martin Van Buren	New York	1782–1862	1837–1841	Democrat	widower
William Henry Harrison	Virginia	1773–1841	1841	Whig	Anna Tuthill Symmes Harrison
John Tyler	Virginia	1790–1862	1841–1845	Whig	Letitia Christian Tyler Julia Gardiner Tyler
James Polk	North Carolina	1795–1849	1845–1849	Democrat	Sarah Childress Polk

Our PRESIDENTS

President	Birthplace	Life Dates	Term	Political Party	First Lady
Zachary Taylor	Virginia	1784–1850	1849–1850	Whig	Margaret Mackall Smith Taylor
Millard Fillmore	New York	1800–1874	1850–1853	Whig	Abigail Powers Fillmore
Franklin Pierce	New Hampshire	1804–1869	1853–1857	Democrat	Jane Means Appleton Pierce
James Buchanan	Pennsylvania	1791–1868	1857–1861	Democrat	never married
Abraham Lincoln	Kentucky	1809–1865	1861–1865	Republican	Mary Todd Lincoln
Andrew Johnson	North Carolina	1808–1875	1865–1869	Democrat	Eliza McCardle Johnson
Ulysses S. Grant	Ohio	1822–1885	1869–1877	Republican	Julia Dent Grant
Rutherford B. Hayes	Ohio	1822–1893	1877–1881	Republican	Lucy Ware Webb Hayes
James A. Garfield	Ohio	1831–1881	1881	Republican	Lucretia Rudolph Garfield
Chester A. Arthur	Vermont	1829–1886	1881–1885	Republican	widower
Grover Cleveland	New Jersey	1837–1908	1885–1889	Democrat	Frances Folsom Cleveland

President	Birthplace	Life Dates	Term	Political Party	First Lady
Benjamin Harrison	Ohio	1833–1901	1889–1893	Republican	Caroline Lavina Scott Harrison
Grover Cleveland	New Jersey	1837–1908	1893–1897	Democrat	Frances Folsom Cleveland
William McKinley	Ohio	1843–1901	1897–1901	Republican	Ida Saxton McKinley
Theodore Roosevelt	New York	1858–1919	1901–1909	Republican	Edith Kermit Carow Roosevelt
William Howard Taft	Ohio	1857–1930	1909–1913	Republican	Helen Herron Taft
Woodrow Wilson	Virginia	1856–1924	1913–1921	Democrat	Ellen L. Axson Wilson / Edith Bolling Galt Wilson
Warren G. Harding	Ohio	1865–1923	1921–1923	Republican	Florence Kling De Wolfe Harding
Calvin Coolidge	Vermont	1872–1933	1923–1929	Republican	Grace Anna Goodhue Coolidge
Herbert Hoover	Iowa	1874–1964	1929–1933	Republican	Lou Henry Hoover
Franklin D. Roosevelt	New York	1882–1945	1933–1945	Democrat	Anna Eleanor Roosevelt Roosevelt
Harry S. Truman	Missouri	1884–1972	1945–1953	Democrat	Elizabeth "Bess" Virginia Wallace Truman

Our PRESIDENTS

President	Birthplace	Life Dates	Term	Political Party	First Lady
Dwight D. Eisenhower	Texas	1890–1969	1953–1961	Republican	Mamie Geneva Doud Eisenhower
John F. Kennedy	Massachusetts	1917–1963	1961–1963	Democrat	Jacqueline Lee Bouvier Kennedy
Lyndon Baines Johnson	Texas	1908–1973	1963–1969	Democrat	Claudia "Lady Bird" Alta Taylor Johnson
Richard M. Nixon	California	1913–1994	1969–1974	Republican	Thelma "Pat" Catherine Patricia Ryan Nixon
Gerald R. Ford	Nebraska	1913–	1974–1977	Republican	Elizabeth "Betty" Bloomer Warren Ford
James Earl Carter	Georgia	1924–	1977–1981	Democrat	Rosalynn Smith Carter
Ronald Reagan	Illinois	1911–2004	1981–1989	Republican	Nancy Davis Reagan
George Bush	Massachusetts	1924–	1989–1993	Republican	Barbara Pierce Bush
William J. Clinton	Arkansas	1946–	1993–2001	Democrat	Hillary Rodham Clinton
George W. Bush	Connecticut	1946–	2001–	Republican	Laura Welch Bush

Presidential FACTS

Qualifications
To run for president, a candidate must
- be at least 35 years old
- be a citizen who was born in the United States
- have lived in the United States for 14 years

Term of Office
A president's term of office is four years. No president can stay in office for more than two terms.

Election Date
The presidential election takes place every four years on the first Tuesday of November.

Inauguration Date
Presidents are inaugurated on January 20.

Oath of Office
I do solemnly swear I will faithfully execute the office of the President of the United States and will to the best of my ability preserve, protect, and defend the Constitution of the United States.

Write a Letter to the President
One of the best things about being a U.S. citizen is that Americans get to participate in their government. They can speak out if they feel government leaders aren't doing their jobs. They can also praise leaders who are going the extra mile. Do you have something you'd like the president to do? Should the president worry more about the environment and encourage people to recycle? Should the government spend more money on our schools? You can write a letter to the president to say how you feel!

1600 Pennsylvania Avenue
Washington, D.C. 20500

You can even send an e-mail to: president@whitehouse.gov

For Further Information

Internet Sites

Find information about Andrew Jackson's childhood:
http://statelibrary.dcr.state.nc.us/nc/bio/public/jackson.htm

Learn more about Andrew Jackson's life and the events of his presidency at the President Andrew Jackson Web page:
http://library.thinkquest.org/12587/contents/personalities/ajackson/aj.html

Find out about Andrew Jackson's papers at the Library of Congress:
http://lcweb.loc.gov/spcoll/127.html

Tour the Jacksons' plantation, The Hermitage:
http://www.hermitage.org

Learn more about all the presidents and visit the White House:
http://www.whitehouse.gov/WH/glimpse/presidents/html/presidents.html
http://www.thepresidency.org/presinfo.htm
http://www.americanpresidents.org

Books

Bealer, Alex W. *Only the Names Remain: The Cherokees and the Trail of Tears.* New York: Little, Brown & Co., 1996.

Feinberg, Barbara Silberdick. *America's First Ladies.* New York: Franklin Watts, 1998.

Ferry Steven. *Martin Van Buren: Our Eighth President.* Chanhassen, MN: The Child's World, 2002.

Rubel, David. *Scholastic Encyclopedia of the Presidents and Their Times.* New York: Scholastic, 1994.

Sabin, Louis. *Andrew Jackson: Frontier Patriot.* New York: Troll Books, 1997.

Index

DATE DUE

DEMCO, INC. 38-2931